# i won't say this aloud

Maya Roberts

BookLeaf Publishing

Presentation by *BookLeaf Publishing*

Web: www.bookleafpub.com

E-mail: info@bookleafpub.com

ISBN: 9789357740616

First edition 2023

*To anyone who craves to be heard.*

*I'm with you.*

# loud yet so silent

it's loud up there;
the area so-called my mind
it's deafening and piercing,
yet still one of a kind.

it's like a personal radio
but nothing i could ever sing to.

no,
it's more like an echo.

it's a reminder of no escape
from everything that i've been through

it's so loud that it's silent

i'm all alone

with this mind

and all of its torment.

# truth be told

truth be told,
caring so much can't hurt you
only when you care more for them
than you care for yourself.

# my love

oh my love
how did we get here?

you're now just a stranger
who i loved so dear

# mindful

they say to be mindful,
but what does that truly mean?

i'm mindful of my skin.
i'm mindful of my body.
i'm mindful of fitting in.
i'm mindful of saying sorry.

my insecurities,
they cling onto me like a leech.
my mind wanders into an abyss;
but that abyss is dark beach.

deep deep waters.
with the waves high and
humanity low.
nothing seen across the horizon,
what matters is down below.

but i'm mindful of my mind.
i'm mindful of my words.
it's these thoughts that i can't escape
and i can't find the right words to say.

i'm mindful that i need help;

i'm screaming out for it.
but i'm mindful you can't hear me
for this beach is deserted
and the water's too endless.

# the love we crave

"i love you."
i fear it's a phrase we neglect
and almost take for granted.
because what love truly means;
well,
that meaning is overly canted.

i can't express this love
nor has it been expressed to me.
is that why i fear it so much?
i don't know what to believe.

maybe i'm incapable of this love
and even unlovable myself
or maybe i expect too much
but isn't love just an expectation itself?

i repeat it to myself
i'm repulsed by my own words.

i can't love anyone
if i can't love myself.
i say my love is endless
but just not with my heart at stake. "i love you."
i fear it's a phrase we neglect

and almost take for granted.
because what love truly means;
well,
that meaning is overly canted.

i can't express this love
nor has it been expressed to me.
is that why i fear it so much?
i don't know what to believe.

maybe i'm incapable of this love
and even unlovable myself
or maybe i expect too much
but isn't love just an expectation itself?

i repeat it to myself
i'm repulsed by my own words.

i can't love anyone
if i can't love myself.
i say my love is endless
but just not with my heart at stake.

# leaving me, leaving you

why did you leave?
it's a simple question
i ask you.

a painful stillness
and a heavy heart
as no answer leaves
your mouth;
so i ask again.

why did you leave?

but the silence is enough
for me to realise

it was me.
i'm the one who left.

# driving solo

i'm driving
i'm dissociated
my conscious mind taking action
the music transports me
it's my safe space away from you

# happy for you

i am empty and alone
but i know not to cry
if i show my tears
then the tears will never cease
so i pretend everything is just fine
pretend everything is alright

because that is what they want to hear because
that is what they need to see

pretend that everything is fine
so that is what they see
and hear
and they continue
to feel the same

# nothing but a dream

time is precious,
but in its place,
i cry for your stare
as i clasp my hands and weep
i thought about you every night
i am but a broken dream

for i may never say goodbye
and i will never say goodnight

# ex soulmates

we had a love so pure
you and i forever
you and i through time
i would have kissed you through time
i shared with you my heart

but our soul was just a mirage
it breaks me
it pains me
we are now just two lonely bodies.

# wasteful

you once promised me an eternity
and so i pray
a cross on the table,
a maroon heart

you once promised me for eternity

give me back my wasted life

# happiness fades

somedays i'm happy
other days i'm not
some of it i try
some of it i don't
some of it just happens
it's hard to put into words
but i do try
i just can't do it all

# a night away

give me a night away,
a day or two.
let's forget this city;
just me and you.

you ask me why,
why i don't want to stay.

in this city
my mind doesn't rest;
but with you
it rests all day.

give me a night away,
it's a tiring battle i face,
you're my only escape
during a night away.

# hope

hope,
a beautiful name of
the grasping, bearing,
clutching, clasping,
unbearable feeling which
we cling onto
in hopes of staying hopeful.
but what does hope actually
mean to us? what is hope
if that's all we have left
to believe in?
what happened to Santa Claus,
the Easter Bunny, the Tooth Fairy?
wishing upon a star never became
so appealing; at what cost?
a tale as old as time to keep us
hanging around.
hope.

# me and you

forever
in the dictionary may mean
a lifetime.

forever
in my language
means me and you.

# above the earth

above the earth i see myself
hiding in the corner.
above the earth i see the world,
it's a place where i don't belong.
it's passing me by;
second by second
and day by day,
oh why am i letting it be this way?

defeat.
i feel defeat.
it escapes me,
leaving a trail for the world to see.
if i can see it above the earth
why is nobody coming to save me?

am i unworthy?
am i invisible?
maybe distant me is the only one
who cares.

above the earth i see myself;
i'm the only one who sees me.
i'm screaming from above,
please find your way out.

but it's time i face the truth,
there's no way out of here.

# within my skin

it's hidden in the cracks
and written in the pores,
indulging my senses
i've never wanted something more.

a love that fills the void;
it's a sickening black hole,
once full of benevolence,
but now an echo in my soul.

pools of tears
and shattered bones.
wasted emotions of
the love i once owned.

it's a newly found complex;
all a branded delusion.
what's embedded within my skin
is all just an illusion.

# out my life

this will be the last you hear from me,
for it is written,
one last hope
blighted, silent
not but an unrequited love
a flickering candle on the table,
a blood red complexion

i'm dearly departed
you're out of my life